GUIDEL

Church
and
Society

*Advocating for
Peace and Justice*

The Reverend Clayton Childers
The Reverend Neal Christie
with Robert Mason
for the General Board of Church and Society

CHURCH AND SOCIETY

Some paragraph numbers for and language in the Book of Discipline *may have changed in the 2012 revision, which was published after these Guidelines were printed. We regret any inconvenience.*

Contents

Called to a Ministry of Faithfulness and Vitality

Y ou are so important to the life of the Christian church! You have consented to join with other people of faith who, through the millennia, have sustained the church by extending God's love to others. You have been called and have committed your unique passions, gifts, and abilities to a position of leadership. This Guideline will help you understand the basic elements of that ministry within your own church and within The United Methodist Church.

Leadership in Vital Ministry

Each person is called to ministry by virtue of his or her baptism, and that ministry takes place in all aspects of daily life, both in and outside of the church. Your leadership role requires that you will be a faithful participant in the **mission of the church**, which is to partner with God to **make disciples of Jesus Christ for the transformation of the world**. You will not only engage in your area of ministry, but will also work to empower others to be in ministry as well. The vitality of your church, and the Church as a whole, depends upon the faith, abilities, and actions of all who work together for the glory of God.

Clearly then, as a pastoral leader or leader among the laity, your ministry is not just a "job," but a spiritual endeavor. You are a spiritual leader now, and others will look to you for spiritual leadership. What does this mean?

All persons who follow Jesus are called to grow spiritually through the practice of various Christian habits (or "means of grace") such as prayer, Bible study, private and corporate worship, acts of service, Christian conferencing, and so on. Jesus taught his disciples practices of spiritual growth and leadership that you will model as you guide others. As members of the congregation grow through the means of grace, they will assume their own role in ministry and help others in the same way. This is the cycle of disciple making.

The Church's Vision

While there is one mission—to make disciples of Jesus Christ—the portrait of a successful mission will differ from one congregation to the next. One of your roles is to listen deeply for the guidance and call of God in your own context. In your church, neighborhood, or greater community, what are the greatest needs? How is God calling your congregation to be in a ministry of service and witness where they are? What does vital ministry look like in the life of your congregation and its neighbors? What are the characteristics, traits, and actions that identify a person as a faithful disciple in your context?

This portrait, or vision, is formed when you and the other leaders discern together how your gifts from God come together to fulfill the will of God.

Assessing Your Efforts

We are generally good at deciding what to do, but we sometimes skip the more important first question of what we want to accomplish. Knowing your task (the mission of disciple making) and knowing what results you want (the vision of your church) are the first two steps in a vital ministry. The third step is in knowing how you will assess or measure the results of what you do and who you are (and become) because of what you do. Those measures relate directly to mission and vision, and they are more than just numbers.

One of your leadership tasks will be to take a hard look, with your team, at all the things your ministry area does or plans to do. No doubt they are good and worthy activities; the question is, *"Do these activities and experiences lead people into a mature relationship with God and a life of deeper discipleship?"* That is the business of the church, and the church needs to do what only the church can do. You may need to eliminate or alter some of what you do if it does not measure up to the standard of faithful disciple making. It will be up to your ministry team to establish the specific standards against which you compare all that you do and hope to do. (This Guideline includes further help in establishing goals, strategies, and measures for this area of ministry.)

The Mission of The United Methodist Church

Each local church is unique, yet it is a part of a *connection,* a living organism of the body of Christ. Being a connectional Church means in part that all United Methodist churches are interrelated through the structure and organization of districts, conferences, and jurisdictions in the larger "family" of the denomination. *The Book of Discipline of The United Methodist Church* describes, among other things, the ministry of all United Methodist Christians, the essence of servant ministry and leadership, how to organize and accomplish that ministry, and how our connectional structure works (see especially ¶¶126–138).

Our Church extends way beyond your doorstep; it is a global Church with both local and international presence. You are not alone. The resources of the entire denomination are intended to assist you in ministry. With this help and the partnership of God and one another, the mission continues. You are an integral part of God's church and God's plan!

(For help in addition to this Guideline and the *Book of Discipline*, see "Resources" at the end of your Guideline, www.umc.org, and the other websites listed on the inside back cover.)

Your Congregation: Transforming the World

As a leader in your local congregation's Church and Society commit-- tee, you have a mission to lead it in engaging the world in transfor-- mative ways. You are called not only to make a difference in the world yourself but also to lead your congregation to make a difference as well. This is an important job.

Love Is the Centerpiece

The cross is the central image of our faith. The vertical pillar reminds us of our connection with the Love of God revealed in Jesus, the incarnate one who comes to live among us. The horizontal bar reminds us of our Christian call to love those around us, to love our neighbors as we love ourselves. The cross, then, presents us a picture of both the love and call of God revealed in the ministry of our Savior, Jesus. "We love because he first loved us" (1 John 4:19).

Love is the centerpiece of our faith. Church and Society ministry grows from this love—our love for God and love for our neighbors—all growing from the love we experience in Jesus Christ.

The World-transforming Mission of the Church

The United Methodist Book of Discipline declares: "The mission of the church is to make disciples of Jesus Christ for the transformation of the world" (¶120). From this we are reminded that our faith is not just about us; there is a greater purpose to our discipleship: the transformation of a trou-bled, broken world. So then we ask, *How can the ministry of Church and Society support the church's world-transforming mission?* Let's explore this question in light of the Bible and our Wesleyan heritage.

If Necessary Use Words
"Preach the gospel always. If necessary, use words."
—St. Frances of Assisi

If love is the essence of the gospel, the way we demonstrate love makes all the difference. Our lives become a sermon; our love becomes our greatest witness.

Painting a Vision of a Promised Future

Some years ago in a conference hosted by the General Board of Church and Society (GBCS), a staff member of an annual conference issued a challenge: "I wish you would talk more about what you are for and not so much about what you're against." While there is certainly a place for stating clearly what the church stands against, it is also true that, often, by stating our positions in positive ways we are able to draw in supportive volunteers who want to do something significant and meaningful. A positive vision invites participation.

Jesus' ministry provides a model for this approach: Jesus repeatedly began his teaching with the phrase: "The kingdom of God is like..." He wanted to paint for people a picture of a promised future. He wanted to invite people to join in the work of making it happen. "This is what the kingdom of God is like..." Now, how do we make that kingdom a reality right now, right here, "on earth as it is in heaven"? Answering this question continues to be the church's challenge today: How do we make the reign of God a reality right now where we live?

Building Relationships

At the center of the gospel is relationship: God's desire to be in restored relationship with a fallen, broken creation. As Christians we are called to be part of this ministry of reconciliation, first by being reconciled to God ourselves and then by becoming ministers of reconciliation in a broken, hurting world. As Christians we are called to bring people together.

Church and Society leaders need to focus attention on building networks of people working for change. So often we can adopt a "Lone-Ranger" approach. We become identified as the "prophetic voice," the "lonely prophet." This is not the model Jesus adopted. Jesus knew real social transformation happens when movements are led by nurturing leaders, leaders who do the work of nurturing other change leaders.

Building relationships is key to successful Church and Society ministries. Who are the key people in your church you need to get to know? Who do you need to know in your district? In your conference? In your community and state? By building these relationships you can help cultivate networks of people committed to making a difference, people who have the assets and power to make change happen.

Prophetic Ministry: Our Scriptural Call

The Ministry of Mirror Holding

One aspect of Church and Society work is simply the hard work of holding up a mirror that allows the church and the community to actually see the brokenness of the world around us. Surely God cannot be pleased with much of the picture in today's mirror. A good first step is simply to look hard at the world, in all of its brokenness, and then pray for help and hope in the midst of it all.

What Does It Mean to Be a Prophet?

Many people misunderstand what it means to be a prophet. Often, people equate prophets with soothsayers or fortune tellers. In the Bible prophets are people called out to be God's messengers, boldly proclaiming God's word in a world gone astray. Prophets lift up a holy vision. They express God's desire for the world. They tell the truth about the world and call for change. Many times this hard work is not appreciated.

Many dozens of stories exist in the Scripture of people fulfilling the prophetic role. Here are a few.

- **Shiphrah and Puah** were two courageous midwives in ancient Egypt. They conspired to defy a law established by Pharaoh that required they kill any newly born Hebrew male babies. This law had one purpose: to wipe the Hebrew people off the face of the earth. Shiphrah and Puah stood up to the Pharaoh and risked their lives by refusing to carry out the king's decree (Exodus 1:14-16).

- **Moses** became a mouthpiece for God, demanding freedom for the Hebrew slaves in the halls of Pharaoh's palace.

- **Esther** is remembered for her courage as she risked her life to go before the king to plead the cause of the Hebrews.

- The prophet **Nathan** confronted King David with God's word of judgment after David had an affair with Bathsheba and had her husband killed.

- **Daniel** refused to obey the order requiring all people to bow down and worship the idol.

• **Jeremiah** warned the people of Jerusalem about their coming defeat at the hands of the Babylonians.

• **John the Baptist,** according to Scripture, was the son of a priest, Zechariah. It was expected that he would follow his father's footsteps and become a priest as well. Instead, he assumed a prophetic role, distancing himself from the religious establishment. He dressed in rough clothes, lived in the wilderness, and proclaimed "a baptism of repentance for the forgiveness of sins" (Mark 1:4). People flocked to him. Surely his popularity and message were threatening to the established priestly class who oversaw the temple. Each day ritual sacrifices were made in the temple "for the forgiveness of sins." What is the ministry of John saying about the ministry of the priests? About their temple rituals? Yet, we see in the New Testament, that from the start, Jesus identified his ministry, not with the temple establishment, but with the ministry of John the Baptist (Mark 1).

Jesus Was Also a Prophet

Jesus is celebrated in the Christian church as God incarnate, the very presence of God in the world. His life and teachings bear witness to God's vision for all people. Jesus' ministry was world-transforming. Because of this, he presented a threat to those in power, especially the religious and political authorities.

No evidence suggests that Jesus ever had any special theological training to assume this role. He was never ordained. His baptism by John the Baptist actually identified him with a movement outside the official temple realm. Still, while not acknowledged as a legitimate leader by those in established positions of power, he was seen as a leader in the eyes of his followers because they could see in him a messenger sent from God.

Prophets in Scripture almost always arise from the masses, not from places of power. They are chosen by God for particular tasks. They are appointed by God for special missions. They bring the world a message from God.

Prophetic Ministry Is a Biblical Calling

The church must not deny its calling to proclaim God's message to a hurting, broken, fallen world. Many times this message is directed at those in seats of power. One does not have to study the Scriptures very long to see that very few of the biblical kings won God's approval. Then, as now, those in power were using their power to benefit themselves and those close to them, rather than for the common good. Power tends to corrupt. Many scriptural passages tell the stories of prophets boldly challenging society and rulers to turn from evil, return to God, to love kindness and practice justice.

Theologian Robert McAfee Brown gives us three guidelines for making an effective prophetic witness. First, where you stand will determine what you see. Whom you stand with, will determine what you hear. What you see and hear will determine what you say and how you act. We are called to be part of a church that stands up alongside forgotten, forsaken, and marginalized people; the people John Wesley called, "Christ's bosom friends."

As we stand with the marginalized of the world, what do we see? What do we hear? What will we say? How will we act? These are the questions we need to ask both in the church and in society if we are going to make disciples of Jesus Christ for the transformation of the world.

Following Jesus Can Be Dangerous

"Jesus got into trouble, and so will we, for attempting to transform society rather than to conform to it. But if we name the Name, and if we are followers of The Way, we are called to engage in the redemption of the social order. We are to help bring healing and wholeness to a broken world."

—The Reverend Dr. George Outen, former General Secretary, General Board of Church and Society

---

A Tradition of Advocacy: Unity in the Ecclesia

The early Jesus movement was called "the Way"—not the Answer and not the Destination. These followers of Jesus were people working out their salvation, seeking to faithfully exercise their religious faith. Frequently they did so in an urban context where Christianity flourished in the center of the Roman Empire.

Christianity was multiracial, multinational, multicultural, and culturally syncretic. It crossed economic and age differences. It brought people together in a way no other religion could.

The biblical word translated in English as "church" is the Greek word *ecclesia*. In other ancient sources this word is used for a political assembly of citizens "called out" to make decisions. It is interesting that ecclesia is the word the early Christians chose to describe their assemblies. The church became a "para-kingdom," people who were citizens of a Kingdom existing "alongside" the imperial kingdom. The church was made up of persons who had been "called out" to be part of the "kingdom of God" movement. The Apostle Paul, though a citizen of Rome, was also "called out" to be part of the church. This community of believers became his ultimate loyalty.

How is the local church a place where allegiances are altered? How is the church today a para-kingdom in the places where we live?

In the books of Acts and Revelation, Christians are "called out" to be a new nation. Their primary identity was to be as members of this new community (John 14:17-21; 16:8-11; 17:13-18). Worship, the sharing of common goods, doing good to enemies, mirrors what happens on the "other side" in heaven.

Mercy and Justice
There is a difference between ministries of mercy and those of justice, acts of charity and prophetic witness. There is a difference between responding to immediate needs with acts of charity and working to change systems that hold people down. The church is called to do both.

What God Requires

"What does the Lord require of you but to do justice, love kindness and walk humbly with your God?" (Micah 6:8). This passage is a pinnacle passage in Scripture. It is one that every follower of God should memorize. One cannot help but be struck by the strong language here: God *requires* this of us.

If we consider the passage in context, it is evident that God is frustrated by people who simply want to "play church." They love the ritual. They love the ceremonies. They love bringing their sacrifices to the altar of God. But God knows their hearts. God knows the way they live the other six days of their week and because of this, God considers their offerings empty, and their worship useless. Scripture says it makes God sick to his stomach.

Wow! This is a powerful message. Is this a danger for us today? Is it possible we may also come together as a church community, go through the motions of worship, while the needs of the poor all around us are going unmet?

Malaria, a preventable and treatable illness, is claiming the lives of more than 800,000 people a year. This is a justice issue! Most of those dying are children under the age of five. The United Methodist Church's "Imagine No Malaria" campaign is part of a worldwide movement to make deaths from malaria a thing of the past.

To do this, we must attack both the illness itself wherever people are infected and the cause of the illness: mosquitoes, which carry the infection. Both are essential. When people get sick they need treatment, but it is also critical that we drain the swamps and put up mosquito nets so people don't get sick in the first place. It is not enough to just treat people after they are sick, we need to attack the root cause of the illness. This is true for other church ministries as well.

Holistic ministry addresses both the symptoms and the root cause.

We will never end poverty by just giving out bags of groceries or money. At times our acts of charity may even serve to sustain a poverty system as time and energy is shifted to responding to the immediate symptoms rather than dealing with the root causes.

Justice requires that we challenge the oppressive system that keeps people in poverty. Poor education, unaffordable housing, lack of access to health care, unfair wages and unemployment are all root causes of poverty. They need to be addressed. Until the root causes are changed, people will not be able to live lives of dignity. They will continue to be dependent on charitable handouts.

Is it better to teach people to fish or to give them a fish? Of course, all of us would say it is better to teach them to fish so they can care for their own needs with dignity. Justice ministry is committed to establishing new systems, new societal structures that allow all people to grow and flourish and reach their full God-given potential.

St. John Chrysostom taught: "When we attend to the needs of those in want, we give them what is theirs, not ours. More than performing a work of mercy, we are paying a debt of justice."

St. Ambrose taught: "You are not making a gift to the poor woman or man from your possessions, but you are returning what is theirs. For what is common has been given for the use of all, you make exclusive use of it. The earth belongs to all, not to the rich."

Our Wesleyan Heritage—Social Holiness

When John Wesley said that there is "no holiness but social holiness" he was warning the church against the practice of isolating itself from the world. There is always a danger of hiding away within the walls of the church while the world is perishing around us. Holiness calls us to be God's witnesses in a hurting world. We cannot hide, for we live not in the isolation of our holy temples but in the world where people are hurting.

The faith Jesus demonstrated is lived out in the world. It is a faith that cares about the needs of the poor, cares about the illnesses of the sick, the nakedness of the unclothed, the oppression of the enslaved, and the loneliness of the imprisoned. Biblical faith is active faith. It isn't reserved for the purity of the holy cloister. It is a faith that rolls up its sleeves and goes into the world to make a difference.

Yet, most Christians fail to make this connection. Church for most Christians is something we do on Sunday. Many create a strong divide in their minds between "church" and "society," the sacred and the secular. Church is the pure sanctuary where we come to be holy. Society is the sinful world where we live the rest of the week.

How can United Methodists become disciples transforming the world if we never bring the church and the world together?

Where did Jesus spend most of his time? The Gospels tell the story of a human Jesus, God indwelling human flesh, living a human life among human beings in a most human way. Jesus knows what it is like to be hungry. He knows what it is like to be betrayed. He knows frustration and rejection. He hurts for those he loves with his whole heart. Jesus is a teacher and his teachings mainly relate the reign of God coming "on earth as it is in heaven."

Jesus wants broken people to experience healing, sinful people to experience love and grace, fallen people to regain their strength and leap for joy. This is the way he lived. These are the lessons he taught. So why would it be any different for those of us who are committed to be followers of Jesus in the twenty-first century. If the church is the body of Christ, we need to constantly measure ourselves by the example of Christ. Are we walking "in his steps"?

Has God changed? Is God less concerned today about the hungry and the oppressed than God was 2,000 years ago. Has God given up on helping the sick or being a friend to the imprisoned? Does God no longer care when rulers oppress their people or the powerful abuse the weak?

The church, if it is to be the body of Christ in the world, needs to act like it. It needs to be revived by the gospel message anew, and see Jesus for who he is. Maybe the church needs to be reborn? Maybe it needs to be healed of its blindness. Maybe it needs to wake up, and look around. Surely, God is not satisfied with the world as it is. The reign of God is just not here yet, a long way from it.

Methodists and the Leveling of Society

"I thank your ladyship for the information concerning the Methodist Preachers. Their doctrines are most repulsive, and strongly tinctured with impertinence and disrespect towards their superiors, in perpetually endeavoring to level all ranks, and do away with all distinctions. It is monstrous to be told that you have a heart as sinful as the common wretches that crawl on the earth. This is highly offensive and insulting, and I cannot but wonder that your ladyship should relish any sentiment so much at variance with high rank and good breeding."

> —Letter from the Duchess of Buckingham to the Countess of Huntingdon, who was a supporter of the Wesleyans

---

Living in the Way of Christ

"If any would be my disciples let them deny themselves, take up their cross and follow me" (Matthew 16:24).

To be a faithful disciple of Christ means to walk in the way of self-denial, living a life of simple devotion, a life dedicated to the love of God and to loving our neighbors as we love ourselves. Is this not the message of the sheep-and-goats story recorded in Matthew 25? Those judged to be pleasing to God are the ones who have spent their lives in service of those in need: feeding the hungry, clothing the naked, visiting the lonely, and so forth. This is a countercultural message in a world dedicated to consumption and materialism. Every day we are bombarded by commercial messages reminding us of what we do not yet possess. We are promised abundant life, rich and full life, if only we will purchase this or that product. Is this the way of Christ? Jesus said: look to the lilies of the field. Life is more than possessions. Faithful prophetic witness requires that we challenge the materialistic culture of our day.

The reign of God on earth as it is in heaven is not about Christians ascending to positions of prestige and power. It is about the way of God permeating all of life, from the least to the greatest, so that all of creation might be blessed and flourish. God wants everyone to enjoy abundant life (John 10:10), but this life comes not in the acquisition of many things but in letting go, surrendering, trusting our lives to the way of Christ. In surrendering ourselves, we find our true selves, we open up, we are transformed, we become part of the new creation as our minds are remade and transformed. In Christ, we assume new ways of living and being in the world. The love of God fills our being and flows through us as we become God's prophetic agents of compassion and change in the world.

John Wesley on Ecology

"But the lesson which our blessed Lord inculcates here, and which he illustrates by this example, is that God is in all things, and that we are to see the Creator in the face of every creature; that we should use and look upon nothing as separate from God, which indeed is a kind of practical atheism; but with a true magnificence of thought survey heaven and earth and all that is therein as contained by God in the hallow of his hand, who by his intimate presence holds them all in being, who pervades and actuates the whole created frame, and is in a true sense the soul of the universe."

—John Wesley, Sermon 23,
"Upon Our Lord's Sermon on the Mount, III"

What Does Justice Mean Anyway?

A youth choir from St. Louis was visiting the United Methodist Building in Washington, D.C. They were asked: What does justice mean to you?

A 15-year-old girl replied, "Justice means making the world look the way Jesus would want it to look if he were here."

Faithful Advocacy and the Local Church

- The purpose of the Church and Society Committee is to make the connection between mercy and justice, and then work for a holistic ministry that includes both. This is a practical theological goal.
- Church and Society leaders are to facilitate the connection between those who are engaged in doing mercy well.
- Areas of focus include: homeless and shelter hospitality; tutoring for children; elders outreach ministry; justice and advocacy ministry; work supporting clean air and water; public policy advocacy at the local; state and national level; ministries concerning alcohol, tobacco, gambling and other addictive behaviors; advocacy for just, humane immigration reform; advocacy to protect civil rights, to end all forms of government-sanctioned torture; and advocacy supporting human rights for all people.

The *Book of Discipline*, United Methodism's book of law, spells out what your congregation can expect from you. Read the sections that relate to your work as Church and Society chairpersons.

As a church leader it is important to:
- keep your church council aware of the needs for study and social action on issues;
- recommend social concerns study and/or action projects to the church council;
- cooperate with other ministry teams in your congregation to survey the needs of the local community and to make program recommendations that will help your church respond to local, community, state, national and international needs;
- maintain contact with district, conference, and general church groups such as the General Board of Church and Society who are also working on social justice issues. These groups can provide resources and support for your work at the local level. They also will learn from you and your experience and be able to share these insights with others.

The *Book of Discipline* is a rich resource to support your local church's Church and Society ministries of Christian social education and social engagement. It is important that you and your team be familiar with the Church's Social Principles (¶¶160-166 of the *Book of Discipline*). The Social Principles provide guidance for your team as you lead the church to act on issues of social concern.

In addition, read the *Discipline*'s section entitled "The Meaning of Membership" (¶¶216–221 of the *Book of Discipline*). Become familiar with the section on "The Function of the Local Church" (¶202 of the *Discipline*) that begins: "The church of Jesus Christ exists in and for the world.... The local church is a strategic base from which Christians move out to the structures of society."

The theme of faithful social outreach is also emphasized in the section on "The Call to Ministry of All the Baptized" (¶220 of the *Discipline*): "Each member of The United Methodist Church is to be a servant of Christ on mission in the local and worldwide community." Christian social advocacy and action are important ways the church can engage and impact the world for good. As a Church and Society leader you are in a unique position to ensure that this critical ministry becomes a reality in your local church setting.

What Does It Mean to Be an Advocate?

The word *advocate* is derived from the Latin root word *vocare*, which means "to call." An advocate can be understood as "one who pleads the cause of another." Advocacy is our calling. We, as Christians, are called to speak up, and to "resist evil, injustice and oppression in whatever forms they present themselves" (United Methodist Baptismal Covenant). By standing alongside those who suffer, we strengthen them, encourage them, and offer ourselves to support and amplify their cries for justice.

It is important that in offering our support we must not disempower those we are trying to help. Sometimes, in our eagerness to serve, we "speak for people" or "do for people" without taking time to hear their story or listen to their perspective. This is so important. Ministry must begin with honest conversation and intentional listening. We must be ever vigilant that our "ministry" not become "majesty" and that our humble intentions not morph into prideful show. So often, even the way we try to help can cause pain and hurt.

Advocacy and Prayer

It is important for you as a Church and Society leader to tend your spiritual life. Advocacy can be draining and discouraging. At times it can be frustrating. We need help from God to do this work. Make time for daily spiritual prayer and enrichment. Share honestly and openly with God the challenges of your life. Pray for guidance in your role as a church leader. Pray for team members by name and pray for the tasks that need to be done.

Also, take time to pray for your church and community. Pray as you read the newspaper. Pray for your community as you walk through its streets. Pray for community leaders and for state, national, and world leaders. Prayer is one way we "walk humbly with God." It helps us keep our work in perspective and it reminds us even to care for those whose positions may differ from our own.

Advocacy and Worship

The act of worship is central to who we are as a faith community. How we conduct worship reveals much about our identity. Do people feel welcome in your local church? Visitors often watch to see if the values the church proclaims are expressed in the way it worships. Be sensitive to roles of leadership during worship: Who collects the offering in your church? Who says the prayers? Who reads the Scripture? Who preaches? Does the worship leadership in your church reflect the diversity of people in your church and community? Do you see diversity of age, race, gender, ethnic backgrounds? Are the hymns and litanies supportive of the denomination's call to be ministers of peace and reconciliation in the world, or do they reinforce violent or parochial images of God?

Advocacy and Missions

People want to be able to act on their faith. Many Christians translate faith into action through volunteering for mission projects in their communities and beyond. People can find a new place in the life of the church through mission trips. Youths can find new meaning in life by taking time from their summer vacations to be involved in voluntary mission service. Such projects offer an excellent opportunity for discussion on the root causes of problems that plague our communities. They can foster an environment conducive to deeper analysis and critical thinking.

Consider these questions as examples: Why is it that so many people in our community are homeless? What does this say about the availability of jobs that pay a living wage? What might this teach us about our community's provision of health-care services? How have poor communities in developing countries been affected by global policies that limit or undermine their economic development? Who benefits from the current system? Who pays the price for these policies? How might current systems be changed so they are more fair for everyone? These questions and others like them are challenging to address, and leaders should prepare carefully to engage others in this discussion.

Careful research can add to the hands-on mission experience by providing an important educational component. How can you support your missions committee in its work of addressing critical needs from a holistic perspective? It has been said that every service opportunity should be accompanied by prayer. It might also be said that every service project should be accompanied by social justice reflection and advocacy.

Advocacy and Christian Education

Education happens every day. We are constantly being formed and reformed. Rather than be tossed about, to and fro, with no purpose, we should direct education to accomplish particular ends. What then is our purpose?

George Albert Coe, a leading figure in the growth of the Christian Education movement once asked: "Shall the primary purpose of Christian education be to hand on a religion, or to create a new world?"

This is a critical question. We need to prepare people not only to be Christian believers but also to be Christian practitioners: people who practice their faith each day of their lives in ways that change the world around them. Education should always be connected to some form of concrete action. Education and awareness on an issue should not be understood as replacing doing justice. We reflect critically on social concerns in light of our Christian faith so we can take action to make a difference. Education, when done well, results in change.

Sometime ago the Roanoke District in Virginia Annual Conference hosted a youth-planned weekend gathering focused on World Hunger. Over 80 youths gathered for an overnight retreat where they committed to fast for 30 hours to better empathize with the hungry of the world. The planning team also made sure that the youths took time to discuss the factors that lead to poverty and malnutrition.

Youths were then invited to write a letter to their congressional representative to express their personal opinion about a bill that would increase the money provided by the federal government to school lunch programs. The small increase would make a big difference by enabling schools to provide more nutritious meals, buy locally grown produce, and develop school gardens in which students would be able to grow their own fruits and vegetables. Several months later youths from the district celebrated when the bill was passed and signed into law by the president.

Advocacy and Evangelism

Many people have written off the church because they have not yet heard the whole message of God. What they know about the church has been shaped by the warped portrayals they see constantly in the media. Many have not yet heard that God passionately loves the world and that we as God's people are called to be faithful stewards of all creation. Many have not yet heard that Jesus Christ is the Prince of Peace and that we are called to be peacemakers, ministers of reconciliation in a world addicted to violence. Many have not yet heard that we as God's people are called to love all of God's creation: inviting and welcoming every person in grace and love to worship and serve God.

We worship a savior who opens his arms wide on the cross, and in so doing proclaims: "There is nothing you can do to me to make me stop loving you." This is the gospel message, God's open invitation that many have not yet heard. How can we reach religion's "cultured despisers," those compassionate but secular people who consider the church at best irrelevant or at worst as an "opiate of the people"? How do we connect with the masses of people who see the church as being preoccupied with "pie in the sky, by and by" and unconcerned about making a difference in the here and now?

We know that this is not the true essence of the church, but many people believe this is who we are.

The General Board of Church and Society hosted a group of 24 students from Africa studying at schools in the United States. We worked with advocacy partners to plan an "Imagine No Malaria Advocacy Day" in which the students were first briefed on the issues and then met with members of the U.S. Congress. The students first thanked the legislators for the generous support given by the U.S. government in the past. Then the students asked for future support in the fight to eradicate deaths from malaria.

As we walked back to the United Methodist Building, a staff member from a partner anti-malaria agency who helped plan the day's visit was asked if he was involved in church anywhere. "No," he said, "but if I ever got involved, I'd want to be involved in a church like this one."

We need to rethink how we do church. Church must be more than a building. It is more than an organization. Church needs to be seen as a movement of people formed by the love of Jesus Christ, inspired by the Holy Spirit, and actively working to renew God's world according to God's will, not ours.

Mercy and Justice

While charity or mercy tends to focus on immediate recognizable needs and short-term answers to long-term problems, justice focuses on long-term change. While charity is often reactive, justice is proactive; it goes "upstream" to address the root cause of issues.

Mercy is optional. It depends on our benevolence, our willingness to help. Justice is not an option. Mercy can be withdrawn from those to whom we offer it whenever we choose. Justice cannot be withdrawn. It ensures that all people are given what they are due. Justice results when we establish social structures that guarantee human dignity and rights. Mercy can include one-time donations for natural disasters, food baskets, or clothes for the homeless.

While mercy is often necessary, it also, at times, can be harmful. There is a danger of viewing people as objects to be tended to, rather than human beings who bear the image of God. Sometimes people giving help make decisions without consulting the very people who will be affected by the charity. This is dehumanizing.

Mercy can preoccupy our time and talents to the point that we are too weary to even imagine a world of justice. The person with a problem is taken care of, but the broken system remains unchanged.

Mercy rarely offends anyone, while doing justice usually offends someone. It challenges unjust systems that benefit some while hurting others. Prophetic advocacy stands with those in need, people crying out for just change. Remember Moses going into Pharaoh's court: He was not asking for charity, he was demanding justice. God was his advocate, standing by him, supporting his cause.

Simply put, justice challenges those who have the power to bring about just change to make those changes. This can take many forms. At times, it may mean marching in the streets to demand change. But it might also mean having a person-to-person, heart-to-heart conversation with someone in power. This is also advocacy, and it may prove just as effective.

Advocacy can mean organizing communities to build capacity and power, so the community can be represented. It can also mean coming together to talk and pray to God for help and guidance. Advocacy may involve boycotting products or services that harm people or, perhaps, purchasing products that help people. Even the purchases we make are a witness to the values we hold dear.

Why Not Church?

Every day we are flooded with news of events throughout the world. We know immediately about the latest demonstrations in Asian capitals, bombings in Middle Eastern cities, natural disasters in South America, and the latest corruption scandals in European governments. We then hear experts share their opinions on a broad range of issues, but where do we go to think about them in light of our Christian faith?

Why not church? Church should be a place where we can be real people, express honest viewpoints, pray about real issues and then try to do what we can to help. This is what it means to be relevant. It means we are real.

Practicing What We Preach
Every church should set a high example in how it conducts itself in the community. Our actions are our witness. People watch how we show hospitality, purchase products, care for our workers, and acquire services. This, too, is a form of advocacy and a witness to truths we preach.

Salvation As Healing

The Greek word *sodzo* often used in the New Testament for "salvation" can also be translated as "healing." This is important to properly understand this concept. For instance, in John 3:17 Jesus says, "Indeed, God did not send the Son into the world to condemn the world, but in order that the world might be saved [healed] through him."

Healing often takes time. Healing involves different prescriptions for different people and different symptoms. Illness is often the result, not of individual failure, but of poor living conditions in the entire community. Holistic healing involves one's whole being, mind, body and spirit. Indeed, holistic healing should not be limited to the individual but should reach out to include one's whole community. How might this understanding of salvation as healing affect the way we do ministry in the church and the world?

Resources to Support Your Church and Society Ministry

Following in Jesus' Steps

Are we following in the footsteps of Jesus if we fail to go out into the highways and byways where he spent so much of his time? Jesus lived among the people and most of his recorded encounters happened in people's homes, in marketplaces, on hillsides, at the seashore. As a church, where is our energy expended? Through faithful community involvement, our commitment to the way of Christ can provide a healthy and supportive influence to a wide variety of community organizations.

Five Steps to Success

As you engage in advocacy ministry keep these goals in mind:

1. **Pray.** Seek God's help and wisdom as you embark on the work of God.
2. **Relate.** Take time to build relationships with other key members of your church and community. Most people will be willing to hear your perspective if you take time to develop a positive, respectful relationship with them.
3. **Educate.** People you work with will want to clearly understand why an issue is important before they are willing to get involved. Take time to lay the groundwork. The more people understand, the more enthusiastic they will be as advocates.
4. **Act.** It is not enough just to study social issues and to discuss them among ourselves. We need to become a part of the public witness and advocacy process. Send a card or letter to legislators. Make phone calls. Write a letter to the editor. Talk to friends and neighbors. Take a stand. Let your voice be heard.
5. **Reflect.** Take time to celebrate and reflect. Talk together about the action, celebrate successes, and take note of ways to improve.

The Cry of the Oppressed

As long as there are some who continue to benefit at the expense of others, people will cry out for justice. Surely God hears their cry. Will the church hear their cry?

Acting Locally While Thinking Globally

In Acts 1, Jesus directed the church to go forth empowered by the Holy Spirit to be Christ's witnesses in "Jerusalem, Judea, Samaria, and to the uttermost parts of the earth." Our mission is local, but it must not stop there. We must also be Christ's witnesses on a state level, a regional level, a national level, and a worldwide level. Jesus Christ came to redeem the whole creation. This must be the church's vision as well.

Measuring our effectiveness must not be limited to considering the well-being of one's own community and neighborhood. It is a travesty if children in our community have access to good health care but children in Africa are dying from treatable diseases simply because they cannot afford to pay for medicine. The church cannot rest until no child dies needlessly. This is the transformation the reign of God demands. Surely God's vision for creation includes the care and healing of sick children.

If the streets in my neighborhood are clean and neat but the community next door is being polluted by a toxic waste dump, then the church still has work to do. Surely God's vision for creation includes a clean environment for all of people, not just the few.

If the crime rate is low in our community but other areas are suffering crime sprees in which dozens of people are being killed, then the church must not rest. We have work to do. Surely, God's vision for creation includes safe and secure streets for all of God's people. This is the ministry of Church and Society: the church engaging a broken world and doing what it can to make it whole.

What Not to Do
Do not lead your church to endorse particular candidates or parties or support them with your church's resources. This could put the congregation's tax-exempt status at risk.

Getting Started: Twelve Ways

1. **Pray** regularly for public servants (local, state, national, international).
2. **Stay informed.** Think critically. As a church leader your faithful witness can inspire others to become informed citizens as well.
3. **Teach** the Social Principles in new-member classes, confirmation, Sunday school, and other forums.
4. **Sign up** for *Faith in Action*, the weekly e-newsletter of the General Board of Church and Society at www.umc-gbcs.org/fia.
5. **Recruit partners.** There are many people who would welcome a chance to make a positive difference.
6. **Lead your team** to focus on particular social concerns important to your church and community. What are they? What can we do?

7. **Organize** an "Offering of Letters" on a particular issue. Bread for the World offers samples of this at www.bread.org. People write their members of Congress to express heartfelt concerns. The congregation dedicates the letters before they are sent.
8. **Host informative forums** at your church. If you invite candidates, invite all the candidates.
9. **Encourage voting.** Democracy only works if people participate.
10. **Host a voter registration booth** at your church to encourage voting. Contact your local board of elections for details.
11. **Discuss and reflect.** What are the issues we need to be concerned about as people of faith? How can we add our voices to the public debate? How can we become advocates for God's Shalom in our community and throughout the world? (See "Communities of Shalom," *Book of Resolutions*.)
12. **Get help.** Who in your local church would be interested in the type of ministry Church and Society offers? Are there people passionate about caring for the environment? Are there people concerned about the needs of the poor? Are there young people eager to work to change the world? Let them know that there is room for them on your team!

A SPIRITUAL WORK—PRAY FOR HELP

Finally, we must remember that Church and Society ministry, like all ministries is at its core a spiritual work. Our best efforts fall short if they are done in our own strength. We need God's help. Surround your team and your work in prayer. Seek the wisdom and blessing of God. Take time to listen.

STEPS TO ACTION

Ever wonder why people don't take action? Why is it that so many people when confronted by clear information about injustice choose to turn away and do nothing? Often a lack of action is caused by a lack of resources. Here is a simple example of one way that you as Church and Society leader could take one issue and move people from awareness to action.

1. **Awareness.** Many people have a vague awareness of the problem but no real sense of the facts or its relevance to their lives. We must find creative connections between the issues we are passionate about and the people we are trying to reach. For example: My niece has asthma and I know it has something to do with the air she is breathing. I want to do something to help her.
2. **Knowledge.** To move people to action we must connect their awareness with knowledge: equip them with facts and information that is accurate

and directly relevant. For example: Power plant pollution in your neighborhood is a direct contributor to poor air quality and increased asthma attacks.

3. **Value/Ethics.** The church must play a critical role in connecting a value, ethic, or moral to the facts. Here we give voice to the values that shape who we are as people of faith. People are more apt to act on information if it touches them on a deeper level. For example: Our faith teaches us to care for creation and for our neighbors. How can we as Christians allow pollution to destroy the earth and harm our brothers and sisters?

4. **Develop Skills.** The next step is to empower people for action, to give them skills they need to act on the knowledge they now have. For example: Provide information on where to purchase compact fluorescent bulbs to reduce energy use, how to switch to green energy options if available, or how to contact elected officials to advocate for tighter emission controls.

5. **Action!** Following steps 1–4, people are equipped to take action. Actions can/should include a range of personal, congregational, and community options for engagement on the issue. With each action comes growing awareness and knowledge so the cycle of steps can begin all over again.

Success Stories

A few years ago a group of concerned United Methodists in Arkansas realized that the state's poorest citizens had not received a cost-of-living raise in almost ten years. It seemed that everyone else's wages were rising each year at least to keep up with inflation, but Arkansas' poorest workers continued to work at the minimum wage of $5.15 an hour. The wage never increased, year after year.

A coalition of people led by a United Methodist pastor, the Reverend Steve Copley, decided to do something to raise the minimum wage. They came together and found they had some strong partners for the task: the conference Board of Church and Society, the bishop, United Methodist Women, other denominational partner churches, the Arkansas Council of Churches, and labor unions. Also a number of business leaders wanted to pay higher wages, but were being undercut by low-wage employers. These all agreed that the minimum wage, $10,712 for a full-time worker who never takes a day off, was far from adequate and should be raised at least $1 per hour.

Some within the state saw such talk as a threat to their profit margins: raising wages for the state's lowest-paid workers would be a hit to their bottom line. Talk of raising the minimum wage was threatening. The campaign determined that the state legislature would not act on the issue and that the best approach would be to present gathered signatures and a referendum directly to the citizens of Arkansas. Volunteers hit the streets and began collecting the thousands of signatures needed to get a referendum on the ballot.

The campaign got a big boost when it was given a $7,000 grant to conduct a survey asking citizens in Arkansas if they believed the minimum wage should be raised by $1 an hour for the state's lowest-paid workers. This was among the best $7,000 ever spent: An overwhelming majority of Arkansans said yes. The success of the survey put the issue high on the state's agenda. Statehouse leaders met with campaign leaders and agreed to a compromise proposal. Then the state legislature quickly acted to raise the minimum wage by $1 per hour.

The governor signed the bill and the wage was raised. Many previously thought that Arkansas was not a state that would take the lead nationally in raising the minimum wage. But because a group of church leaders and their community partners felt a strong urging to take on this issue, the political pundits were proven wrong.

What Does the Church Say?

"Since low wages are often a cause of poverty, employers should pay their employees a wage that does not require them to depend upon government subsidies such as food stamps or welfare for their livelihood."

—*United Methodist Social Principles* ¶163.IV.E

COMMUNITY CENTER

Led by the Reverend Stephanie Ahlschwede, Dietz Memorial United Methodist Church, a 65-member congregation in downtown Omaha, Nebraska, launched the Blue Flamingo, a multifaceted neighborhood-based nonprofit that includes a thrift store, fair trade, community garden, and literacy and arts programming.

FAIR TRADE MARKETPLACE

Manchester United Methodist Church in St. Louis, Missouri, started a Fair Trade Market four years ago with a handful of volunteers, a few tables of items and big desire. Today the market has become the largest annual all-volunteer Fair Trade Market in the United States. It is a widely anticipated event in the St. Louis metropolitan area.

Fair Trade provides developing-world artisans and their families quality of life income for the course of a year. The gains are a life of dignity and worth earning fair pay for fair work. For the family this often means more than one meal a day, a chance for children to attend school, access to health care, work in safe environments away from sweatshops, and ability to smile with pride for a job well done.

VOTER REGISTRATION

People are marginalized in large part because they do not know how to mobilize the power of their voice and vote. The Reverend Glen "Chebon" Kernell Jr. as senior pastor of the Norman (Oklahoma) First American United Methodist Church orchestrated the "Rock the Vote Campaign," an effort to use music and celebration to encourage youth and Native American voter registration.

ALCOHOL AND DRUG ADDICTIONS

Trish Merrill founded Faith Partners, which has merged with the Rush Center of the Johnson Institute. Faith Partners is a step-by-step approach to initiating a lay ministry to address both prevention of alcohol and drug problems and addiction recovery support.

HANDS-ON MISSIONS AND PRESERVING DIGNITY

Many Christians catch their first glimpse of the kingdom of God on a mission trip. With time apart to seek and serve God, they experience the power of Christ's presence. Too often, however, trip participants miss an important dimension of the kingdom: God's call to contribute to the building of a more just world.

When Hurricane Katrina hit at the start of his second year of his ministry, the Reverend Cory Sparks led a team of pastors responsible for five churches in the New Orleans Mission Zone to develop strategies for mission workers. These strategies include encouraging missioners to recognize Christ's presence in the community and in the people they meet; respecting the people they serve and their leadership abilities; understanding the social dynamics of race, class and gender in the mission context; moving beyond mercy to justice by catching a vision of God's transforming power in a community; and identifying ways to support communities through political advocacy and other justice work.

Special Sundays for Church and Society

Worship also offers an excellent opportunity for the people of God to join with United Methodists throughout the world in special worship offering and service themes that support Church and Society ministry. How many of these did your congregation celebrate last year? Are there things you can do to promote these special services for next year?

Human Relations Day, the Sunday before the national observance of Dr. Martin Luther King Jr.'s birthday, strengthens United Methodist outreach to communities in the United States and Puerto Rico, encouraging ministries of social justice.

Peace with Justice Sunday, first Sunday after Pentecost, enables The United Methodist Church to have a voice in advocating for peace and justice through a broad spectrum of global programs. Because of the special offering received on Peace with Justice Sunday, global outreach through the General Board of Church and Society and annual conference-related peace with justice ministries transform lives.

OTHER SPECIAL DAYS THAT SUPPORT CHURCH AND SOCIETY WORK

Festival of God's Creation/Earth Day Sunday, the Sunday closest to Earth Day, April 22, is a collaboration of the General Board of Church and Society cooperating with the National Council of Churches Eco-Justice Working Group to produce Festival of God's Creation resource materials to help congregations celebrate and promote stewardship of God's creation.

United Nations Sunday is the last Sunday of October. The General Board of Church and Society United Nations and International Affairs office prepares special resources to support the observance. These resources may be used by local churches, Sunday schools and adult study groups. For the entire month of October, focus is on the joint campaign by the U.N. Fund for UNICEF. The General Board of Church and Society provides materials to support Trick-or-Treat for UNICEF and the denomination's Imagine No Malaria campaign.

Global HIV/AIDS Day (December 1) affirms our unity with brothers and sisters throughout the world suffering from and ministering to those suffering with HIV/AIDS. We not only provide health care to the afflicted but also work to change public policies that inadequately address HIV/AIDS.

Worship Resources

Members of the Methodist Federation for Social Service, later called Methodist Federation for Social Action, authored and secured adoption of the first Social Creed by the Methodist Episcopal Church at the 1908 General Conference. It was used as a model for social creeds adopted by the National Council of Churches, the Methodist Protestant Church, and the Methodist Episcopal Church, South and other mainline denominations.

THE SOCIAL CREED (1908)

The Methodist Episcopal Church stands:

For equal rights and complete justice for all (people) in all stations of life.

For the principle of conciliation and arbitration in industrial dissensions.

For the protection of the worker from dangerous machinery, occupational diseases, injuries and mortality.

For the abolition of child labor.

For such regulation of the conditions of labor for women as shall safe guard the physical and moral health of the community.

For the suppression of the "sweating system."

For the gradual and reasonable reduction of hours of labor to the lowest practical point, with work for all; and for that life.

For a release from employment one day in seven.

For a living wage in every industry.

For the highest wage that each industry can afford, and for the most equitable division of the products of industry that can ultimately be devised.

For the recognition of the Golden Rule and the mind of Christ as the supreme law of society and the sure remedy for all social ills.

That historic first creed was updated in 1972 following the merger of The Methodist Church with the United Brethren. It remains the social creed of the denomination. It is recommended that this statement of Social Principles be continually available to United Methodists and that it be emphasized regularly in every congregation, such as frequent use in Sunday worship.

OUR SOCIAL CREED

We believe in God, Creator of the world; and in Jesus Christ, the Redeemer of creation. We believe in the Holy Spirit, through whom we acknowledge God's gifts, and we repent of our sin in misusing these gifts to idolatrous ends.

We affirm the natural world as God's handiwork and dedicate ourselves to its preservation, enhancement, and faithful use by humankind.

We joyfully receive for ourselves and others the blessings of community, sexuality, marriage, and the family.

We commit ourselves to the rights of men, women, children, youth, young adults, the aging, and people with disabilities; to improvement of the quality of life; and to the rights and dignity of all persons.

We believe in the right and duty of persons to work for the glory of God and the good of themselves and others and in the protection of their welfare in so doing; in the rights to property as a trust from God, collective bargaining, and responsible consumption; and in the elimination of economic and social distress.

We dedicate ourselves to peace throughout the world, to the rule of justice and law among nations, and to individual freedom for all people of the world.

We believe in the present and final triumph of God's Word in human affairs and gladly accept our commission to manifest the life of the gospel in the world. Amen.

The 2008 General Conference approved a worship litany to be added to the *Book of Discipline* as a "companion" to the Social Creed. The litany was developed after consultations in Central Conferences around the world.

A Companion Litany to Our Social Creed

God in the Spirit revealed in Jesus Christ calls us by grace
  to be renewed in the image of our Creator,
  that we may be one
  in divine love for the world.
Today is the day
  God cares for the integrity of creation,
  wills the healing and wholeness of all life,
  weeps at the plunder of earth's goodness.
And so shall we.
Today is the day
  God embraces all hues of humanity,
  delights in diversity and difference,
  favors solidarity transforming strangers into friends.
And so shall we.
Today is the day
  God cries with the masses of starving people,
  Despises growing disparity between rich and poor,
  Demands justice for workers in the marketplace.
And so shall we.
  Today is the day
  God deplores the violence in our homes and streets,
  rebukes the world's warring madness,
  humbles the powerful and lifts up the lowly.
And so shall we.
  Today is the day
  God calls for nations and peoples to live in peace,
  celebrates where justice and mercy embrace,
  exults when the wolf grazes with the lamb.
And so shall we.
Today is the day
  God brings good news to the poor,
  proclaims release to the captives,
  gives sight to the blind, and
  sets the oppressed free.
And so shall we.

Other Helpful Resources

General Board of Church and Society. Website: www.umc-gbcs.org

How to Engage in Faithful Advocacy. Flier available from General Board of Church and Society at www.umc-gbcs.org/store

Faith and Facts Cards. Four-color, worship bulletin-size cards that address a variety of subjects. Topics include health care, domestic violence, criminal justice reform, HIV/AIDS, human trafficking, death penalty, climate justice, living wage, alcohol and other drugs, gambling, hunger and poverty, and U.S. immigration. Available at www.umc-gbcs.org/store.

Social Principles Booklets. *United Methodist Social Principles* accompanied by a study guide. Order through www.cokesbury.com.

The Book of Discipline of The United Methodist Church. Pay particular attention to the sections on local church ministry and General Board of Church and Society. Order through www.cokesbury.com.

The Book of Resolutions. Published after each General Conference session, and available at www.cokesbury.com.

Justice in Everyday Life. By Howard J. Mason and Neal Christie (Nashville: Discipleship Resources, 2007. ISBN: 9780881774917). Instruction on how to teach the Social Principles.

Living Faithfully Series. Available at www.cokesbury.com.

Your District Office. Many have a district Church and Society committee or equivalent. Find out how you can support one another.

Your Annual Conference Office. Get to know the staff person assigned to Church and Society ministries.

National Council of Churches in Christ. Visit www.ncccusa.org.

Sojourners. Visit *www.sojo.net.*

Ecumenical Advocacy Days. Annual gathering hosted each spring in Washington, D.C., is organized by Washington denominational offices and the National Council of Churches of Christ. Includes visits with legislators on Capitol Hill. Visit www.advocacydays.org.

Lake Junaluska Peace Conference. Organized and run by a grassroots cadre of United Methodists and several interfaith partners, the conference is an annual gathering of people of faith concerned about peace and justice. It is held each fall at Lake Junaluska Retreat Center in North Carolina.

Local Church Grants. The United Methodist Church provides many opportunities for local churches, organizations, and individuals to apply for financial assistance. The opportunities vary in amount, eligibility and purpose. See www.umc-gbcs.org for details, deadlines and applications.

United Methodist Seminars on National and International Affairs

UM Seminars have been enriching lives for generations and can be a vital part of your church's Church and Society ministry. These seminars are educational, interactive, faith-forming, thought-provoking, and fun. A seminar is tailor-made for each group, which selects the topic. The design team at the General Board of Church and Society creates a seminar to answer questions, challenge assumptions, and open the group to reflection on the chosen issues. Recent topics include hunger, immigration, peace, racism, and health care.

Everyone is welcome to participate in the seminars, which are engaging for any age group, from youth to adult.

Washington, D.C., seminars take place at the United Methodist Building on Capitol Hill, adjacent to the Supreme Court and the U.S. Capitol. New York City seminars take place at the Church Center for the United Nations across the street from the United Nations headquarters. Often, seminars include "field trips" to places that connect participants to the seminar theme.

Interested in learning more about seminars?

• For Washington, D.C., seminars sponsored by General Board of Church and Society, call (202) 488-5609.
• For United Nations seminars sponsored by United Methodist Women, call (212) 682-3633.

NOTES

NOTES

NOTES

NOTES

NOTES

_____

_____

_____

_____

_____

_____

_____

_____

_____

_____

_____

_____

_____

_____

_____

_____

_____

_____

_____

_____

_____

_____

_____

NOTES

NOTES

_____

_____

_____

_____

_____

_____

_____

_____

_____

_____

_____

_____

_____

_____

_____

_____

_____

_____

_____

_____

_____

_____

_____

_____